Elizabeth,
It was
a pleas-
to Know y
to Know Thanks fo &
you Lynn

Caregiver Tsunami

Lynn Alexander

Edited by
Alice Ashby Roettger

PublishAmerica
Baltimore

© 2010 by Lynn Alexander.
All rights reserved. No part of this book may be reproduced, stored in a retrieval system or transmitted in any form or by any means without the prior written permission of the publishers, except by a reviewer who may quote brief passages in a review to be printed in a newspaper, magazine or journal.

First printing

This publication contains the opinions and ideas of its author. Author intends to offer information of a general nature. Any reliance on the information herein is at the reader's own discretion.

The author and publisher specifically disclaim all responsibility for any liability, loss, or right, personal or otherwise, which is incurred as a consequence, directly or indirectly, of the use and application of any contents of this book. They further make no representations or warranties with respect to the accuracy or completeness of the contents of this work and specifically disclaim all warranties including without limitation any implied warranty of fitness for a particular purpose. Any recommendations are made without any guarantee on the part of the author or the publisher.

PublishAmerica has allowed this work to remain exactly as the author intended, verbatim, without editorial input.

Hardcover 978-1-4512-0139-0
Softcover 978-1-4512-0138-3
PAperback 978-1-4512-4489-2
Hardback 978-1-4512-6956-7
PUBLISHED BY PUBLISHAMERICA, LLLP
www.publishamerica.com
Baltimore

Printed in the United States of America

Dedication

This book is dedicated to my mother who personifies all that a caregiver can be. She is an inspiration to me and to all who know her.

Acknowledgements

I'd like to thank Ruth LoPrete, Cherie Mollison and Kathy Gnau for their significant contributions to this endeavor. Your dedication and belief in this book were instrumental in its journey to publication.

Foreword

At last we found the "Dear Abby" of caregiving. In her book Caregiver Tsunami, Lynn Alexander provides us with touching, funny, poignant and most of all, practical and helpful advice. Lynn combines her expertise in interpersonal communication with her expertise in aging to clearly describe some of the major challenges those caring for older relatives face; from the health care system, their other family members, and the care recipient themselves. Lynn uses her own poignant and powerful caregiving experiences to illustrate her points; with grace, humor and love. This book will lead caregivers to the right approaches for a better and more meaningful experience for all involved!

Peter Lichtenberg, Ph.D.
Director of Wayne State University Institute of Gerontology

CAREGIVER TSUNAMI
INTRODUCTION

"The Age Wave" was a phrase coined by Ken Dychtwald, Ph.D., to describe the phenomena of our aging population in America. He stated as this Age Wave swept our shores, it would have significant implications not only demographically but for our society as a whole. As a result, we are now experiencing a tsunami effect. For every senior or vulnerable person there are a number of caregivers involved. Every family in America is dealing with the joys and challenges of caring for a loved one. Thus, the Caregiver Tsunami.

It may begin for you in a sudden and dramatic fashion with a startling middle-of-the-night phone call. Or it may occur in a more insidious fashion as you observe the physical and cognitive decline of your parents as they age. Whatever form the role of caregiver takes, chances are we will all assume it sometime in our lives.

Throughout our lives we promise: "I'll Take Care of You." In our wedding vows we pledge to take care of each other "for better or worse, in sickness and in health." When we first gaze upon our newborn child we promise: "I'll Take Care of You." When it comes to birth order, older brothers and sisters are told to look out for their younger siblings.

When we are thrust into the role of "Caregiver," this vow: "I'll Take of You" takes on new meaning. You will find yourself meeting new challenges and facing many roadblocks that will test your patience and your sanity. Being a caregiver is one of the most heartbreaking yet fulfilling experiences of our lifetime. Selfless love and devotion carries with it its own reward, and many achieve an intimacy with their loved ones for which they previously may not have found time. In my case, many wonderful memories were created via my parents' relationship with my son, their only grandchild. Yet as I've become more involved with caring for my parents, I have had time for one-on-one conversations and bonding as never before.

Sometimes this new intimacy comes in the form of a single gem like experience. Several days prior to my mother-in-law's passing, she emerged from being an Alzheimer's patient for one brief, shining moment. During that time, she was lucid and connected. This final farewell proved to be a very healing experience for my husband.

Others report that they learn about talents and memories never before shared and that they relate to their parents in a new way as a person, not just as a parent. This positive aspect of caregiving can be heightened if we become effective in carrying out our role.

Caregiving can be especially stressful for hard-charged leaders who are used to controlling their environments, being decisive and knowing the lay of the land. Over the years I have received many calls from judges, CEOs and community leaders who have become overwhelmed by their new roles as caregivers. They have experienced the Caregiver Tsunami.

This book will help you to ride the waves without drowning by identifying the lay of the land, breaking through road blocks and taking decisive action. You will gain control of your caregiving situation. Never in your life has it been more important to be strategic in your actions.

As a result, you will reduce the stress of caregiving and gain control of your situation. Caregiver Tsunami will provide a roadmap for creating the best possible experience for you and your loved ones.

LAY OF THE LAND

If you are a caregiver, you are not alone. In America right now, there are an estimated 50 million caregivers of various types. The first of the baby boomers turned 65 in 2008; and as they age, the number of caregivers will increase dramatically. Throughout our history we have experienced the Manufacturing Age, the Space Age and the Information Age. We are now embarking on the Longevity Age. Some researchers now predict that there are people alive today who could reach the age of 150. Most people tell me they are only interested if their quality of life matches their age.

With the aging of our population, we see this experience called caregiving all around us. In coffee shops and corner bars, conversations turn from finding homecare for our parents to dealing with the latest knee surgery. Several recent experiences brought this home for me. At a black tie affair, I found myself in the ladies' room calling to check in on my parents. Several other attendees were doing the same. In previous years we would have checked in with our children's sitter. Then, on a return plane trip from Florida, I observed the quintessential male baby boomer in the seat ahead of me. Tan and fit, he was wearing a baseball cap with some gray locks of hair sneaking out from under it. He appeared to be successful, self-assured and full of life. In a caring voice he was reminding his dad that he would be away for a few days on a business trip but that he would call him every day and visit as soon as he returned. So caregiving issues are not simply senior issues. They are family issues, community issues and societal issues.

Affluence and fame cannot insulate us. Caregiving is one of life's great equalizers. Many celebrities and political leaders have written about their caregiving experiences. Some have become spokespersons for organizations which assist seniors.

Aging parents are not the only people who can require care. There are many faces of caregivers within my own circle of family and friends. They can include a husband caring for his wife, a wife caring for her husband, a woman taking care of her husband and father while helping with her grandson, 60-something parents of a 20-something Down Syndrome son, young parents with an autistic child, the mother of a grown son with Lou Gehrig's disease managing his care in another state, parents who have buried several sons, and a grandchild helping with the care of his grandparents. For the purposes of this discussion, we will focus on elder care, whether the person be a spouse, parent, aunt, uncle, neighbor or friend. Whatever the situation, there exists a variety of caregiver roles. They include:

PRIMARY CAREGIVER

As a Primary Caregiver, you are the point person for all care and decisions. You are the one on whom everyone depends. Another way to look at this is through the analogy of a general contractor. Building a house without having someone in charge would be foolhardy. The same is true for the caregiving experience. Through the years, this role had usually been filled by an adult child, often a female relative. Today caregiving has become a family affair involving sons, husbands, grandchildren and neighbors.

SECONDARY CAREGIVER

A Secondary Caregiver assumes the role of an "assistant" of sorts who supports the Primary Caregiver. This may involve filling in, helping out here or there, or taking on specific projects such as doing the taxes or researching care and housing options. There can be several Secondary Caregivers. If this is the case, the-more-the-merrier. It's important to be in sync with the Primary Caregiver to prevent confusion and gaps in care.

LONG DISTANCE CAREGIVER

In this role, the Caregiver manages care and support for a loved one from a geographic distance. There has been a dramatic increase in the number of Long Distance Caregivers across America due to the career demands and mobility of recent generations. While serving as the director of the Michigan Office of the Services to the Aging, I found that the greatest number of hits on our website came from Long Distance Caregivers—during work hours.

If you are also an adult child of your loved one, you may move back and forth between a Primary and Secondary role. Although you are ultimately responsible for your parents, it is extremely difficult to manage care on a long-distance basis. Here is where friends and neighbors can become intimately involved in a group caregiving mode.

THE SANDWICH GENERATION

With the advent of the baby boomers, this term has become more high profile. Many boomers had their children later in life. In addition, their parents are living longer despite the challenges of chronic conditions. Thus, boomers sometimes find themselves caring for parents while still rearing their children. One may begin to feel like liverwurst in a tightly packed sandwich! Or as my columnist friend Kathy Hutson likes to say: "It's the Panini Sandwich Generation".

As if these roles aren't demanding enough, the emotional aspect of caregiving, along with the interactions of others, adds to the mix. It becomes a significant life event when we assume the role of caregiver for our parents. Some folks like to call it "role reversal". Yet it's far more complex. Our parents are grownups who deserve to be treated as such and who should be allowed to retain as much independence as possible. Achieving that delicate balance of child/caregiver is a constant challenge.

From the moment children are born a journey begins of building a relationship between them and their parents. The early years are marked by joys, accomplishments and a need for parents to guide the way. During the teen years there is often conflict and a redefining of roles as children still need the love and guidance from their parents, but are inclined to rebel in some ways. Often what is natural and essential for their growth can be difficult for parents to accept. To add to the joy are many moments of pride and bonding as parents observe the growth and accomplishments of their children. Proms, graduations, weddings and the birth of grandchildren all add to the wonderful mix.

As parents age and they begin to need some assistance of their own, a new relationship forms. This can be tenuous and a bit difficult since parents may be the ones who rebel now, wanting to maintain their independence as much as possible. Adult caregiver children who were used to having their parents be there for them are now thrust into the role of helping their parents. Many folks talk about this shift as a "role reversal", yet it is far more complicated. Parents are still the parents and children are still their children.

Added to the roles of Primary or Secondary Caregivers is the "cast of characters" surrounding us in the form of siblings, in-laws, neighbors, friends and the professionals.

IT'S ALL ABOUT RELATIONSHIPS

We all know that relationships play an important role in life, no matter what we are trying to accomplish. Stories abound in the work place and are played out in cartoons and television sitcoms. The most dramatic emotional ties happen in families. Hence the popular phrase "Friends are the family you choose". Just attend any family reunion to get the picture. With our children we endured the school relationships as well. Now, as caregivers, we experience the challenge of relating to a slew of medical practitioners and service providers. And those tricky family dynamics come into play ever more.

These relationship dynamics get acted out in the form of maneuvers which get in the way of effective caregiving. Most likely you will recognize many of these maneuvers:

I'VE GOT A SECRET

This game is played by aging parents. Because they don't want to be a burden or because they fear loss of independence, they withhold information. Thus, you could have a situation where, say, an ambulance is called to their home. They refuse to go to the hospital, and you don't find out about it until days later. Or there may be problems with their bills piling up. Perhaps they are having difficulty using the stove with the resultant risk of fire. A policeman once told me that his mother had gone without hot water for days until his sister arrived for an overnight visit. Or they may continue to drive unsafely. One senior who stopped driving was quoted as saying: "It wasn't all that bad, except for the double vision!"

I'D RATHER DO IT MYSELF

Often this game is acted out by a senior and goes hand in hand with "I've Got a Secret". They will try to do everything for themselves and not ask for help. I've been told many times that 80-somethings are still doing their own yard work, or cleaning gutters and falling off ladders.

It is interesting that this game also can be played by Caregivers who form what's called a "symbiotic relationship", where the Caregiver and the person receiving the care become so emotionally intertwined that they are almost one person. The Caregivers lose themselves in the process, cut themselves off from their normal activities and believe that no one can provide caregiving as well as they can. One of the most important programs developed under my tenure, as a government leader, was to expand respite care and adult daycare on a 24/7 basis.

SIBLING RIVALRY

Remember fighting for the front seat of the family car? Residual sibling rivalry can rear its ugly head and get in the way of smart caregiving, becoming a negative distraction and possibly preventing finding of consensus on important issues. This results in wasted time and indecisiveness. Often the most organized and responsible person and/or the dominant sibling takes charge. Siblings may harbor long-held resentments and believe they are being bullied just as they were when they were growing up. Many people believe that when siblings quibble over family possessions, it's because of greed. That may be true in some cases. However, it's my theory that often the underlying motive has more to do with affirming that their connection to their parents was as strong as that of their brother or sister. This takes on epic proportions in blended families.

WHY CAN'T YOU BE MORE LIKE YOUR SISTER/BROTHER?

This game goes hand in hand with Sibling Rivalry. Parents pit siblings against each other and stoke the flames of rivalry. In some cases, the same sibling is the "Golden Child" throughout. In others, roles keep changing; and the siblings never know when they will go from being the favored child to the one who does not measure up. Often the parent will give information to one child and withhold it from the others, who in turn, begin to believe that a conspiracy is taking place.

CINDERELLA'S STEPMOM

Rivaling the antics of Cinderella's evil stepsisters, blended families can wreak havoc, especially with elder law issues. Judges and attorneys can cite numerous incidents of extremely bad behavior—fighting over finances and resources. Often players will try to smear each other publicly and with mutual friends. This can erupt into civil war. You've probably heard: "Where there's a will, there's a relative."

In one case, a woman filed for divorce after only a few years of marriage. She had come into the marriage with minimal assets. The husband had considerable assets. She proceeded to use the divorce proceedings as estate planning for her daughters' benefit. Her request was that her two daughters receive 50% of the trust funds with his three children sharing the remaining 50%. Nice try! As you might imagine, the judge was not impressed with these courtroom antics. This gives new meaning to "Step Monster"!

THE HOT POTATO

Years ago, when I was attending Cub Scout parent meetings, I was often amazed at the skill of many fathers who managed to stare straight ahead, not move an inch and hold steady when a request for volunteers was made. Soon the mothers would start to squirm, and their cheeks would flush. Finally, one or two would raise their hand. In all fairness, male parents helped in many ways. But the memory of that ability to play "hot potato" without getting burned remained with me through the years.

That same game gets played out by families. In most cases, one person emerges as the "Point Person". He or she has grabbed the hot potato. This happens even to people with many siblings. Often this person is labeled as "the responsible one" or the "organized one" and thus is anointed. Although it makes sense to have one person in charge (once again, much like a general contractor), this becomes a GAME when everyone else sloughs off and doesn't carry his or her share of the load. This reminds me of the old class team assignments when you found yourself doing your partner's work. As one primary caregiver put it: "I feel like I missed a family meeting and was elected without my knowing."

THE LITTLE RED HEN

This game is an extreme version of the hot potato. The offending parties do little or nothing to help with caregiving but give face time and share in the glory. In "The Little Red Hen", some chicks did not want to do the planting, reaping or baking. They just wanted to eat the bread. In like fashion, some siblings just want to claim the family antiques or show off for others by doting on their parents when others are around. This dynamic is similar to that of the non-custodial parent who showers their child with fun and gifts while shunning responsibility.

OUT-OF-TOWN EXPERT

Caregiving experts warn to be on the lookout for this game, especially if you are a Primary Caregiver with long-distance siblings. True enough; it is impossible to become intimately involved in the caregiving process if you live out of town or, worse yet, out of the state or in another country. With this game, the "out-of-town expert" comes to visit and then criticizes the decisions and modus operandi of the Primary Caregiver. My rule is that the Primary Caregivers get final say unless their judgment endangers the life or resources of the loved one. Because Primary Caregivers are most impacted by the decisions made (i.e., location of assisted living facilities, surgical outcomes, etc.), they should have the final say as the "general contractor."

ONLY YOU

According to the lyrics of this song, "Only You Can Make the World Go Round". This goes hand in hand with "I'd rather do it myself". Remember when your children were young and they would cry whenever you would try to leave? They were sending the message that you were the only one who could console them or meet their needs, and, let's face it, you liked that. We knew, however, that it was not wise to promote such symbiosis, a psychology term used to describe an unhealthy relationship. Two people become so intertwined that they are like one person. The resulting dependency and denial of individual needs create an unhealthy situation for both people. And it is not healthful in caregiving, either. You don't need to do it all yourself. Even more, both patient and caregiver need a break from each other.

AGEISM

We are all familiar with the novelties which make fun of old age. Although this in good fun, its not so humorous when it gets played out in a serious manner. Ageism runs rampant in our society. It's perhaps the only "socially acceptable" prejudice remaining in our culture. And it never becomes more evident than in our health care system. The most disgusting form of Ageism occurs in the field of long-term care. Some health care professionals assume that patients can't make progress simply because they are old and suffer multiple problems. In one instance, a physical therapist cruelly stated that "Dad" had been nothing more than a "mat" (in other words, a lifeless blob of nothing) since he had begun to work with him. As a result, the therapist rarely made an attempt to get the resident out of bed, choosing the easy way out of exercises in bed. Interestingly, within a few days of working with a new physical therapist, the resident was dressed, sitting up for as many as five hours per day, and even walking 20 feet. A coincidence? I think not!

Other examples of Ageism occur in hospitals. From ER physicians to intake social workers, many health care professionals assume that anyone over 80 years of age is confused and unable to comprehend information. They will talk to the family as if the person weren't there. In our family's case, my son still holds a grudge against a particular ER physician who interacted with his grandfather in this manner. On the other hand, at 85, Mom is very sharp intellectually and very independent, chuckled when a well-meaning waitress once asked if I needed to cut Mom's meat for her!

The following example would be comical if it weren't so pathetic! A foursome of vital athletic women in their 80s enjoyed a typical day of golf then made a stop at a nearby mall, leaving their golf clubs in the trunk. When they returned to look for their car, it was nowhere to be seen! They were almost as upset over the missing clubs as they were the missing car! Immediately, the gals found a security guard and alerted him that their car had been stolen. Looking them up and down and noticeably observing their gray hair, he took on a caring, yet patronizing tone and said: "Are you sure you just didn't forget where your car was parked?" To which they replied: "We had the spot memorized and did a thorough search before contacting you." At his insistence, they drove around the entire parking lot to be certain. Once the security guard was convinced that they were correct, he finally called the local police.

Ageism is running rampant in our society, and it certainly impacts treatment and caregiving situations. Be alert and challenge Ageist assumptions when you or your loved ones experience them.

THE NURSE IS VERY BUSY

We all know of experiences when a rude sales clerk treats us badly while shopping. They may send us the message that they don't care about our business and are too busy to give us the time of day. I have witnessed that very same type of response in the caregiver field. In one instance, a Caregiver asked about a certain medication that had not been administered to a resident on time. "Do you just wait and give it later?" she inquired. Two nurses and/or aides shared a "look right through you" stare and glare and one replied in a "How dare you" tone of voice, "The nurse is busy!"—never answering the question, and never acknowledging the Caregiver's concern.

THE REVOLVING DOOR

This is a systems game. The players are Medicare and its insurance companies. In one case, because of Medicare rules, a senior citizen went from one hospital to another hospital, then to a nursing home and back to the original hospital during a 2 ½ week timeframe. Not only was this a traumatic experience for the patient, it was costly in its own right in terms of ambulance rides, discharges and admissions.

For years I have heard about the "3-week Conspiracy". This means that after three weeks it becomes burdensome for a nursing home to keep someone under acute status. The billing and documentation become more difficult, and they try to push patients into a private-pay situation. Much of the pressure comes from Medicare and insurance companies. Over the past few years, folks have begun to complain to me that they have been told their loved one "is not progressing adequately" and must switch over to private pay or leave. And in every case, I'll bet you can guess how long they'd been there. You got it—three weeks! And I have more bad news: A loved one who suffers from Alzheimer's or any other form of dementia is not covered by Medicare from day one. The reason? "Since they can't understand instructions, they are not capable of progressing adequately."

THE OSTRICH SYNDROME

We've all heard about that famous "ostrich with its head in the sand". Well sometimes it's an entire family of ostriches. Over the years my office has received thousands of calls from these clueless folks. Denial had gotten in the way of preparation. The pleas ranged from "My dad's in the hospital, and we have 24 hours to find a nursing home" to "My mom needs assisted living. Can you help me find who pays for it?" We all know that decision-making under duress is stressful and ineffective. Yet our culture is in such a state of denial regarding aging that many caregivers are having to pull their heads out of the sand to face very difficult situations.

TOO MANY DOCTORS IN THE HOUSE

Just as you can have "too many cooks in the kitchen" you can have "too many doctors in the house" (or hospital). In the case of my father-in-law, all of the specialists were stepping on each other's toes and creating chaos. When we asked his regular physician to take charge of the process, everything went much more smoothly. Experienced caregivers tell me that it is important to have a patient advocate with you as much as possible during a hospital stay. If you are incapacitated or in a weak physical state it will be difficult for you to advocate and track details which may be important for your quality of care. Medical professionals often relate stories of miscommunication between doctors and other problems which occur during the change of shifts. As patients and caregivers we must be constantly be vigilant to make sure that proper medications are given and a plan for discharge will go smoothly.

THE MAZE

Our community has a school farm that hosts a corn maze at Halloween. Children take delight in the confusion of it all as well as the challenge of figuring it out. Deciphering the "maze" of health care and aging services is not as much fun for those of us who are caregivers. The good news is that there myriad services and organizations are available that do provide quality care. The difficulty comes with accessing that care. As a lively senior citizen stated at a Wellness Expo: "Honey here's the problem. I have 15 refrigerator magnets advertising 15 numbers. Which one do I call?"

TAKE DECISIVE ACTION

So, at this point you are probably asking: "How do I deal with all of this and take action?" We can't control everything that comes our way, but we can conquer most problems and regain control by becoming a smart caregiver.

Balancing your role as a caregiver along with interpersonal relationships will become much easier if you take decisive action and employ smart strategies.

The following actions will allow you to do so:

BE VIGILANT

Situations can change quickly overnight or even by the hour. Pay attention to physical symptoms, cognitive changes and relationships. This is particularly tricky for Long Distance and Secondary Caregivers. Many times matters can sound okay over the phone; but once family members come for a visit, they can see that a situation has gone into crisis mode. In one case, a long-distance brother reported that he had just talked with Dad the other day, and he seemed fine with taking care of Mom. Shortly after that, the Primary Caregiver brother replied that since that time their mother had become incontinent and belligerent regarding personal grooming. In reality, their dad had reached his limit within that 48-hour period.

In another instance, a mother complained that her foot was hurting. This was not unusual. However, within a 24-hour period her condition worsened into an extreme case of cellulitis and infection. This resulted in a hospital stay that could have been prevented. Constant vigilance is key, particularly with chronic conditions. Act quickly and decisively. Don't wait to call a doctor or to intervene regarding a quality of care issue. Move quickly to apply for assistance and programs. You may be able to prevent a hospitalization or a further downslide by doing so.

PLAY OFFENSE INSTEAD OF DEFENSE

Encourage the purchase of long-term care insurance, and the checking out of housing, legal and other services before they are needed. Over the years, I've received many calls from people stating: "We are in a family crisis. What do we do?" Once someone becomes hospitalized it is very difficult to obtain a Durable Power of Attorney. Witnesses cannot be family members or hospital employees. If your loved one becomes incapacitated, a situation can become even more complicated. Therefore, prevention is key. Make sure that legal work is taken care of before a crisis occurs. In addition, encourage your loved one to maintain good nutrition, prevent dehydration, maintain medication compliance and prevent falls.

HOLD PEOPLE ACCOUNTABLE

Sometimes it will take a third call or e-mail to get a response. A shining example of this happened with the U.S. Postal Service. When my parents moved from one locale to another, they wanted to continue the service of mail delivery directly to their door. It is required by law in cases of extreme physical hardship, and it had been provided at their previous location. Three phone calls and one on-site visit with proper documentation later, their request was approved. There's an old saying that "The squeaky wheel gets the oil." It is trite, but it's a true statement.

MANAGE FAMILY RELATIONSHIPS

Make sure that your spouse or parents let you know what their wishes are—if they are able. Plan ahead as a family and work together. "Contract" who will do what. And because all Primary Caregivers will be impacted most by the choices that are made, Secondary Caregivers should support their decisions. In addition, Secondary Caregivers need to check their emotions and behaviors. Too often I hear remarks that the Primary Caregiver is bossy just as he or she always has been (sibling rivalry). Secondary Caregivers should recognize that those feelings of resentment may actually be residual responses from long ago. Primary Caregivers need to be careful not to ignore their marital relationship. Partners of Primary Caregivers will experience stress as well. Give and take is extremely important. And in like manner, it will take patience on the part of spouses to support their partner. All of those involved should practice active listening.

PRACTICE STRESS MANAGEMENT

It is a given that life can be stressful. And distress (the inability to handle stress effectively) can even cause health problems. Our immune systems become weak due to what's called the "Fight or Flight Response." You may have heard of strange cases where someone is able to lift a car to save a trapped child or in other cases perform a "miraculous" feat. Of course, these are extreme cases of the "Fight or Flight Response".

You have probably heard the term "survival of the fittest". Our bodies developed the "Fight or Flight Response" as a way to survive as a species. During cave man days, the major stressors were physical in nature: saber-toothed tigers, flood, fires, and attacks by neighboring tribes. The "Fight or Flight

Response" allowed us either to fight off the attack or flee. When this response kicks in, our bodies go on alert status. Our breathing rate speeds up, muscles tense, adrenaline increases, blood pressure increases so that we can react to the situation. Once we take action, our bodies then can go back to a relaxed state, the calm and quiet mode. In cave man days this may have worked well. After all we did survive as a species. The trouble is, today's stressors are quite different. I've seen a lot of strange things in my day on the expressway. But I've never seen a saber-toothed tiger; and I'm betting that you haven't either.

Today's stressors are more intangible, things such as noise, traffic, pollution, deadlines, relationship issues, financial problems, etc. Caregiving is the Big Kahuna of stressors! Personally, in one year I became an empty nester, Primary Caregiver and a menopausal woman. Talk about stress!

Managing their stress effectively will help caregivers remain healthy. The simple act of laughing can help us to relax. Perhaps you've experienced being with a group that is a bit uptight. Then someone tells a great joke and everyone relaxes. This is the power of laughter and humor.

We can also burn off stress through real physical exercise. Moving back to a relaxed state can calm us too. Yoga and meditation are effective tools; and therapeutic massage can help. Many senior centers/community centers are on to this. Most now have some form of wellness center or programs as part of their organizations. Just about every city, village and township in America has a center. Don't be afraid of the title "senior center". Many 50 somethings are now enjoying walking trails, warm pools and Pilate's classes thanks to these beautiful centers. Some are intergenerational in nature. One young man talks about going with his grandma to "her club".

ASK FOR HELP

If you are the Primary Caregiver, it's easy to fall into the game "I'd Rather Do It Myself", especially if others are playing "The Little Red Hen". Don't fall into that trap! Ask others to share the load. Everyone can contribute in some way. And, if you are a Secondary Caregiver, be sure to thank your Primary Caregiver. If you are able, send him or her on an all-expense-paid trip while others provide care. On a lesser scale, provide a rejuvenating visit to a local spa. Gift certificates for an evening out are also an excellent way to offer support.

RAISE YOUR FRUSTRATION TOLERANCE LEVEL

Notice, I did not say "Lower your expectation level." We must still have high expectations and demand quality. You will find, however, that things often don't go as smoothly as we'd like. Glucometers may not work. Visiting nurses may be running late. Pharmacies will run out of medications. You may find out that a prescription comes due the day after the doctor's appointment. Or you may find yourself in "voice mail purgatory" being switched back and forth like a yo-yo while trying to find services.

If you are impatient in nature and have a low frustration tolerance level, this becomes a nightmare for you. Still, expect the best but don't let the frustrations get to you. Take a deep breath and go with the flow! Practice moving to relaxation. You may find yourself thinking that you can't take anymore. Tell yourself: "I can handle this."

CALL IN THE PROFESSIONALS

Think about it. None of us would try to do surgery on ourselves. And we all call in professionals for everything from car washes, house cleaning, hairstyling, taxes, legal work and landscaping. So don't try to do it all on your own when it comes to caregiving. There are many public sector, government and service agencies that can guide you to help. In addition, if your family is having difficulty in reaching consensus on key decisions, you may want to use the services of a mediator. For Long Distance Caregivers and those with little time, a care manager can act as the general contractor for you. Home care providers can provide needed respite. Hospice services can ease the burden of end-of-life care. Technology can assist also. Personal emergency response systems, medication management products and sensor alarms for loved ones with dementia or Alzheimer's are lifesavers.

RELISH YOUR CAREGIVER ROLE

This advice comes from my husband. He was a Primary Caregiver for his mom with Alzheimer's and his dad who had leukemia. His exact words were: "Tell them to enjoy being a caregiver because they will miss them (their loved ones) when they are gone." Because the caregiving experience can be stressful, it is easy to fall into the trap of becoming overwhelmed and focusing on the negative. Be sure to capture those moments that are precious gems and treasure them. Join in family games that were a part of growing up. Interview your folks and do an autobiography. Share family memories that have added to your sense of self.

Here is a personal example: One spring afternoon I became overwhelmed by that first smell of lilacs in a beautiful neighborhood setting. I flashed back to my childhood neighborhood. I was blessed with a fun and loving neighborhood—with lots of birthday parties, plays, badminton and baseball games in the yard. The backdrop was beautiful small-town American yards flush with roses, lilacs, maple and apple trees. I immediately called my parents and thanked them for providing me with such a wonderful childhood experience.

Rummaging through possession of long ago, a fire truck or favorite doll, may provide great memories and the opportunity for conversation.

BECOME A CHAMPION FOR COMPASSIONATE CARE

There is a lot of great care out there, but also a lot of bad care. An important part of creating change must be our willingness to become a Champion. Caregivers—As caregivers we can use our Decisive Action Step: Be Vigilant. Observe your surroundings; take note of how care is provided to others around you when *their* family members are not present. Check for signs from your loved one. Pay attention to physical symptoms. Ask questions; talk with the physician, nurse, social workers, aides and physical therapist. Just be there! Be around enough to know what's going on. Be assertive. If things aren't going as they should—speak up.

Many people who have experienced numerous hospital stays go so far as to say: "Have an advocate with you 24/7." Although this is an admirable goal, it is not always practical. However, there are many other things you can do as the caregiver. First of all, know your loved one's rights. Medicare, insurance companies and nursing homes all must adhere to standards that ensure those rights. Every state has an Office on Aging, which will provide you with information. They also provide a Long-term Care Ombudsman program. Don't be afraid to call them.

That being said, it's usually best to go through "appropriate levels" before calling in the state. Your best ally is the physician and the social worker. Often a physician will take a stand with an insurance company or Medicare to benefit his or her patient's recovery. Likewise, a social worker is usually a compassionate professional who understands your concerns, has the most contact with various professionals, and can exert a strong influence.

If these steps don't work, your next course of action should be to request a meeting with the director of a nursing home or the nurse care manager of a hospital setting. Keep working your way up the organizational ladder until you get the desired results. If you are not successful, then it is important to call the ombudsman and/or the appropriate regulatory agency.

Communication styles are an important part of successful intervention. Blame or personal attacks result in defensiveness. Be specific with your requests and ask many questions. Do not cave in, however. Be persistent and firm. Make sure they know that, although you hope to resolve it here first, you will take it to the next level if necessary. You will deal with situations where hot dogs and corned beef are given to patients on a low-salt diet, sugar will be given to diabetics and your loved one's calls may go unanswered for an unacceptable period of time. Be armed and ready with your advocacy. Hold people accountable. I recommend that patients have a friend or relative with them as much as possible during a patient's hospital stay and that a log be kept of tests, treatments and consultations.

Professionals—check yourself. Make sure you aren't suffering from "compassion fatigue." Remind yourself to:

Look *into* the person's eyes rather than looking *through* them.

Listen with your whole heart.

Touch them with compassion; don't just touch them to do something to them. Unfortunately, most of the touching seniors receive comes in the form of shots, blood pressure checks and drawing blood.

USE POSITIVE COMMUNICATION

The noted psychologist Albert Moravian created the concept of "Communication Cues" or messages that we give to others through our verbal and non-verbal communication. These include:

Verbal—The words or content of our message

Vocal—The voice tone, inflection, pitch volume and rate of speech

Visual—Our body language

We often can give incongruent (mixed) messages. We all know folks who say "We need to have teamwork" when they really mean "You need to do what I want." Or we all have seen public speakers whose message is lost because of their poor posture or poor eye contact. Not to mention the ones with the shrill voice tones!

As caregivers we want to send congruent and positive messages to our loved ones that provide dignity for them. Using the term "briefs" instead of "diapers." Saying "It's important for you" as opposed to "You have to do this," or "You can't do that" can help to soften a situation. Stating "Let's talk about (something positive) or bringing in jokes and articles is far better than confronting them for complaining. When the time arrives to move from their home call it "rightsizing" instead of "downsizing".

When it comes to voices, talking loudly enough without shouting at them is key. Speaking slowly enough and enunciating clearly is also important. Be sure not to mumble. Also, if you are feeling a bit worn out or perturbed, you may be experiencing "compassion fatigue". If you're not careful, you will reveal this in your tone of voice. Take a deep breath and get some respite for yourself the first chance you get so that your loved one won't feel that he or she is a burden.

Visual messages are also important. Be sure to look right into their eyes, twinkle and smile. Beyond these communication cues let's talk about touch. As was mentioned before, much of the touching that is done to older people is clinical and even painful in nature. Their temperature and blood pressure are checked. If they are diabetic, their finger is pricked to test their blood sugar. A myriad of tests is performed on a constant basis. So it's very important as caregivers that we touch with love and compassion. Hold their hand, remember to hug them, brush their hair and soothe their forehead. When I cleanse my dad's face, I tweak his nose in a playful, loving way. It never fails to bring a smile to his face no matter what kind of day he's having. Stories abound regarding the healing touch of compassionate nurses. Our positive communication can be every bit as healing in nature.

BE AN EARLY BIRD

During our formative years we were told: "The Early Bird gets the worm!" This is ever so true when it comes to caregiving. A waiting line for assistance at the Veterans Administration can grow from three people at 9:00 a.m. to 12 or more people by 10:00 a.m. An afternoon physician appointment can be delayed by previous schedule challenges. This creates "The Domino Effect".

If your loved one receives a new prescription, you must walk it into the pharmacy. Sometimes mishaps can occur late in the day. If the pharmacist cannot read the writing or does not understand the instructions, it may be too late to reach the physician's office. Or the pharmacy may be out of a medication, particularly if it is a controlled substance. You may find yourself driving across town to an affiliated pharmacy to gain access to the coveted prize. Not to mention that after 5:00 p.m. those lines become long with tired, cranky commuters and sick children who just want to get home. My advice: Show up early and try to book appointments early in the day if possible.

Using these strategies will help you become a smart caregiver.

Armed with knowledge, you will make smart decisions, which will save time, money, resources and frustration. Most important, knowledge will help to create the most positive and enduring caregiving experience for you and your loved ones. This will free you up to enjoy your relationship. And, in turn, your loved ones will respond. It will make things easier for them.

MANAGE FAMILY RELATIONSHIPS

Make sure your parents or spouse let you know what their wishes are. Plan ahead as a family. Everyone should get together to talk about how you will work together. "Contract" who will do what. And all Secondary Caregivers should work to support decisions of the Primary Caregiver since they will be impacted by choices made. Partners of Primary Caregivers will be under stress as well. Give and take is very important here. Primary Caregivers need to be careful not to ignore their marital relationship. And it will take patience and support on the part of the spouse. Who shouldn't sulk or pout and should pitch in and take on some of the tasks his or her partner usually performs. The Caregiver then will be more likely to have the energy to play and have some fun.

DO YOUR RESEARCH

We hear many stories about insurance companies not covering certain costs. However, you may be surprised that everything from ambulance transportation to lift chairs might be covered. In one case a long-distance ambulance trip was required from one hospital to another. Everyone said that it would be outrageously expensive. When we checked, the co-pay amount was actually quite minimal. In another situation, we were told that the nursing home resident would be covered only for around 90 days. Upon checking, we were told that the insurance company would pay for up to six months of care, given that progress could be made. Don't assume anything. Check out what coverage is available.

On another note, applying for reimbursement can be quite complicated. It's been noted that death and taxes are two of the most difficult things to deal with in life. Understanding Medicare should be added to this list. Another challenge can be lack of preparation. If you can get ahead of the game and be ready for challenging situations before they strike you will be more in control and less vulnerable to the Tsunami effect.

To get you started, here are some answers to frequently asked questions:

ANSWERS TO FREQUENTLY ASKED QUESTIONS

1. What are Medicare and Medicaid?

Both Medicare and Medicaid are government programs that provide assistance to the sick and the needy. Medicare is health insurance for senior citizens who are 65 or older and under 65 years of age for certain disabilities. Medicaid provides medical assistance to low-income individuals. Some citizens are "dually eligible" meaning they can access both programs. At this time only Medicaid pays for long-term care. Thus, you must "spend down" your assets until you have met the requirements for Medicaid in order to receive assistance with paying for long-term care.

2. What is Long-Term Care planning and why would I need it?

With our increase in longevity, comes the chance that at some point in our life we will need assistance with activities of daily living (grooming, chore services, medication assistance). We are often unprepared to pay for this assistance. We can avoid the need to spend down our reserves and end up on Medicaid if we plan carefully. Purchasing long-term care insurance and planning for our older years is an essential part of life planning. One of my best legacies as director of the Michigan Office of Services to the Aging was to lead my office in creating a long-term care insurance benefit for State of Michigan employees. Its one of the best things employers can do for their employees and its so important that individuals are advised to purchase this insurance on their own with an individual policy if necessary. Check with your state office on aging for further information.

3. What is a Durable Power of Attorney and why do I need one?

A Durable Power of Attorney allows persons to name someone to manage their financial affairs if they are unable to do so. A Medical Power of Attorney allows your representative to make sure your wishes are followed with regard to medical care and procedures. Many folks do not realize the importance of these documents until they find themselves in a hospital or nursing home situation. At that point it becomes much more difficult to complete the paperwork because it requires a notary public and two witnesses, neither of which can be a relative or an employee of the facility. If you suffer a cognitive decline, it becomes much more complicated and involves court proceedings. Planning ahead is the name of the game here.

4. When does a person need a guardian?

A person needs a guardian when he or she becomes physically, mentally or financially unable to function independently. The issue of a need for a guardian can come up in a variety of different ways. Sometimes the family might be worried that Mother is leaving the stove on all the time, or she can't properly write out checks to pay the bills, or perhaps she bought magazines she did not need, or made large contributions to a charity that she cannot afford to support. The issue can come up if mother is admitted to the hospital and the hospital is worried that she does not understand the medical treatment they want to perform. Often a nursing home declares that a guardian must be appointed in order for her to be admitted. Sadly, sometimes one sibling is worried that another sibling is taking all of the mother's money and they want to put a stop to it.

In each of these cases it is really important to try to determine what would be accomplished by seeking a guardian. Guardianship takes important rights away from a person that we all take for granted. Therefore, it should be used only as a last resort.

It is important to know exactly what a guardian is. The following definition and list of alternatives is taken from the website of the National Guardianship Association at www.guardianship.org. This website provides valuable, reliable and in-depth information about guardianship and should be consulted if you are considering it.

Definition: Guardianship, also, referred to as conservator ship, is a legal process, utilized when a person can no longer make or communicate safe or sound decisions about his/her person and/or property or has become susceptible to fraud or undue influence. Because establishing a guardianship may remove considerable rights from an individual, it should be considered only after alternatives to guardianship have proven ineffective or are unavailable.

Alternatives to guardianship may include:
- Representatives or substitute payees
- Case/care management
- Health care surrogacy
- Trusts
- Durable Powers of Attorney for property
- Durable Powers of Attorney for health care
- Living wills
- Community advocacy systems
- Joint checking accounts
- Community agencies/services

Clearly defining why you think a guardian is needed will help determine which of the alternatives to guardianship listed above might work instead. For example, having a guardian will not ensure that Mother will turn off the stove. This might more properly be addressed by finding a good care management program that would define needs and help bring in the kind of assistance needed for Mom to safely conduct activities of daily living like cooking and self care.

Finding a representative payee for Mom's Social Security check, or a money management program could help Mom pay her bills and provide her with counseling about not buying things or making contributions she cannot afford. Or, Mom might be happy to have a trusted family member help with paying the bills. Do not overlook the fact that the real issue may be that someone selling magazines or soliciting for a charity is taking unfair advantage of your mom. The family needs to stop them and let them know that you will be watching. Community advocacy systems can help you if that is the real problem that needs to be solved.

Every area of the country is served by a state or local area agency on aging. The area agency will be able to provide more information about all the programs mentioned above. Contact information for them can be found in most local phone books under aging services and/or area agency on aging. Web-based search engines such as Google and Yahoo can locate area agencies on aging and other aging services by using those key words and the name of the applicable state and local areas for the search. The Elder Care Locator hotline is (800) 677-1116 which will help to find local aging programs and services nationwide.

A number of the other alternatives to guardianship listed above such as Powers of Attorney, trusts and health care surrogacy need to be drawn up when the person is still able to make sound decisions. Everyone should consider these documents at any age because one never knows when an accident or illness will strike and the person could become unable to make his or her own critical life decisions. Most attorneys can create these documents or refer a person to one who does.

Planning ahead and having these documents prepared is the best thing families can do to avoid heartache and headache in the future. These documents and decisions must be made with the full consent of the older adult, and ideally with the full participation of all the other involved family members.

The possibility that a family member may be taking unfair advantage of a parent or older relative is often a reason the other family members go to court to seek a guardianship. If this is really happening, it is probably a matter for the police to investigate. It is always morally wrong and usually illegal. Some police agencies and prosecutors are very willing to take these cases others are not unless what is happening is really serious and really evident. Even in these cases, the problem you are trying to address is the action of the family member and that is what needs to be fixed.

Families also need to be very clear about the motives behind asking for a guardianship. When one family member wants a guardianship of a parent to gain control of the life and property of the parent, the other family members usually object. If this matter goes to court and the parent is found to need a guardian, the court often has no choice but to appoint an independent, professional guardian and the family can lose all control and involvement in the life choices and property of the parent during the parent's lifetime.

In the event that a hospital or nursing home requires that a guardian be appointed for a parent, the family has the right to ask very specific questions about why. The most basic question is: Why do you believe my parent cannot make informed decisions about his or her own care? The answer that the nursing home is worried about its legal liability may or may not be a good reason to seek a guardian.

Most adults over age 65 have Medicare that helps pay the cost of their in-patient hospital care. As Medicare beneficiaries, they have rights and responsibilities related to hospital care. Every state has a Peer Review Organization (PRO) that answers questions about those rights and responsibilities and can provide more information about options if the hospital is demanding a guardian and you don't agree. Contact information for the PRO is often found in the Medicare notices provided at admission or by contacting your state office on aging.

The question above also applies in the event a nursing home is demanding a guardian for admission to the facility, or at other times during your parent's stay. Fortunately every state has a long-term care ombudsman program that can help you sort out whether or not a guardian is needed. The ombudsman programs can be located through the Elder Care Locator and the state or local area agency on aging.

Finally, guardianship is sometimes the right thing to do if none of the available alternatives solve the problems or meet the needs of your loved one. The following is a list of duties of the guardian outlined on www.guardianship.org.

Guardianship of the Person

When the court appoints a guardian of the person, the guardian may have the following responsibilities:

- Determine and monitor residence
- Consent to and monitor medical treatment
- Consent and monitor non-medical services such as education and counseling
- Consent and release of confidential information
- Make end-of-life decisions
- Act as representative payee
- Maximize independence in least restrictive manner
- Report to the court about the guardianship status at least annually

Guardianship of the Estate or Property

"Estate" is defined as real and personal property, tangible and intangible, and includes anything that may be the subject of ownership.

When the court appoints a guardian of the estate, the guardian is assigned the following responsibilities:

- Marshal and protect assets
- Obtain appraisals of property
- Protect property and assets from loss

- Receive income for the estate
- Make appropriate disbursements
- Obtain court approval prior to selling any asset
- Report to the court on estate status

If the court determines there is a need for a guardian and you choose to take on that role, it would be very useful to review the resources for guardians on the www.guardianship.org website. The site also points you to local professional guardians and guardianship associations that might be able to provide training and education for family guardians. The court, usually called Probate Court, can also help you understand how to ask for the appointment of a guardian. In addition, some courts provide training and education for guardians.

5. How does one find suitable housing?

Our home is one of the most important elements in our lives. Hence, the popular sayings "Home is where the heart is," "I'll be home for Christmas" and "Honey, I'm home" strike a chord in us. For seniors, especially, moving from the home in which they've resided for years can be traumatic. Planning ahead and creating excitement can help to alleviate this. For instance, talking about the experience as "rightsizing" instead of "downsizing" is key. Some factors to consider are:
- Privacy
- Separate entrance
- Proximity to the Primary Caregiver
- How capable is the person(s) with regard to activities of daily living?
- Available transportation
- Supportive services
- Quality of care
- Staff retention rates
- Testimonials from residents and their families
- The ability to age in place

Check out the options in person. Senior residences not only

give tours, they will invite prospects to lunch or dinner there. Also, most senior centers hold Housing Fairs and Expos where many places can be checked out at once and options can be narrowed down. Chances are four or five places will seem appealing for site visits. Remember that this is the time they are trying to make their best impressions. If there are red flags in terms of communication or environment trust your instincts.

6. What is a CCRC?

A CCRC is a continuing care retirement community which allows a person to age in place. In other words as their needs progress on a "continuum of care" (i.e., independent to assisted living to nursing home care) they can remain on the same campus. This can also prevent further stress and uncertainty. It also makes friends and family more comfortable because they don't have to keep changing locations for their visits.

7. What are the latest trends in housing?

One of the most innovative types of housing and long-term care services can be found in "The Eden Alternative." Created by Harvard-trained physician Bill Thomas, it is a new way of providing long-term care as opposed to the "old nursing home up on the hill." Eden Alternative residents enjoy a homelike atmosphere. They can care for their pets and plants when able to do so. They have a mailbox. In other words, they are home. An Eden home is a place to go to live instead of a place to go to die. It provides a new standard of care called resident centered. Residents and their families call the shots rather than having to fit into the more structured criterion of the old "medical model" of care. For more information go to www.edenalt.com.

8. When should I encourage my parent(s) to obtain a geriatric assessment?

Once again, trust your instincts. Do you or others around you have concerns regarding memory, mobility, balance, grooming, paying of bills, naiveté regarding sales calls or scam artists?

Has your loved one(s) become disengaged from life and other people? Do they seem depressed or tired? Have they stopped engaging in activities that they once enjoyed? Have they expressed any concerns about finding their way home from events? If any of these are true, it makes sense for your loved one to seek a geriatric assessment. That way you'll know if it's still safe for them to live independently or continue to drive.

Too many times people try to live in their home on their own for too long. Horror stories abound regarding people who have fallen and can't get help. In one instance, an elderly woman had just been visited by a senior companion. The visitor had brought fruit to her and left it on her nightstand alongside her bottled water. The homeowner fell and she was not found for several days. She managed to survive on the fruit and water until she was found. What if that visitor had not come that day? Again: Be vigilant, be proactive and seek out an assessment if there is the slightest doubt.

9. How do I go about arranging for an assessment?

Many hospitals and universities have geriatric departments with reliable assessment capabilities. Geriatricians may also be able to carry out an assessment within their practices. Your Area Agency on Aging and many county offices have nurses and social workers who can do basic assessments with referral to specialists.

10. How do I persuade my parent(s) to stop driving?

Are you worried about your parent(s) driving? If so, you are not alone. So often we hear from adult caregiver children that they don't know how to get their parents to stop driving although they know that it is no longer safe for them to do so. Why is it that otherwise sensible seniors hold so tightly to their car keys at the risk of harming themselves or others? Everyone craves independence and dignity. If the keys have to be yanked from their hands that is even more the case.

Many seniors are still quite capable of driving. Others are in total denial that they aren't capable. If you are worried about your parent(s) safety, it is important to have a conversation with them sooner as opposed to later. Don't wait until they have had an accident involve your parents in the decision-making process. Perhaps you can talk about the fact that they have lived a good life and have always shown good judgment. Encourage them to take a senior driving assessment so that they can make an educated decision about continuing to drive. In many instances there are skills they can learn in order to stay behind the wheel. If not, it is important to let them know that you won't leave them stranded. Alternative transportation is very important. Also, don't try to do a role reversal and become the parent. They are still your parents and should be treated with respect.

Put yourself in their shoes. All of us can remember when we passed our driving exam or got our first car. That sense of independence. One creative family held onto the car keys for their 90-year old dad, but they left the car in his driveway. Once a week they would sit in the car with him in the driver's seat just so he could remember what it was like. They did a great deal of bonding and reminiscing during those "drives."

If they still insist on driving, you may be able to gain the support of your family physician. Sometimes parents will listen to outsiders rather than to their children. Often it is difficult for adult children to have these types of conversations. The "Generation Gap" can still have an impact beyond our teenage years and create roadblocks to comfortable conversation. By following some simple strategies we can ease that discomfort.

The Area Agencies on Aging also have excellent information on early planning, communication and skills assessment. For further information go to: www.n4a.org (Area Agencies on Aging).

11. Where can I go for help as a caregiver?

If you are a caregiver it is essential to get support for yourself. Too often caregivers try to do it all on their own and end up with caregiver burnout. This can lead to exhaustion, medication errors, health issues and compassion fatigue. With compassion fatigue, a caregiver can become impatient and irritable. This is not good for your loved one or for you. Having someone fill in for you and give some much needed respite, as well as peer support, can be extremely useful in these situations.

One of my best legacies as a Michigan cabinet official was the expansion of respite care statewide and a 24/7 service. Also, the expansion of adult day service with grooming facilities allows caregivers to still be a two-career family. Your state office on aging, Area Agency on Aging or senior center can help you find respite care. Also, private home care companies can be a tremendous help. Be sure to use a reputable company that is dedicated to training and screening of their caregivers. Ask if the owner or administrative staff accompanies the caregiver on his or her first visit. Do they conduct regular customer satisfaction surveys? What is their policy if a caregiver is absent? Make sure they do background checks on their employees. Having someone come into your parents' home raises their level of vulnerability. Make sure they are safe and protected.

12. How can I check out the quality of care at a prospective nursing home?

Unfortunately many families play the Ostrich Game with their heads in the sand. Thus, they often do more sound research for finding a hair stylist or dry cleaner that they do for selecting a nursing home. Since they haven't prepared ahead, a family may be confronted with a situation where the hospital notifies them that they have 24 hours to find a nursing home for their parents or one will be chosen for them. This is yet another situation where it's far better to be prepared. Check out nursing homes ahead of time. Use the same selection strategies we talked about under the housing question. To check out any quality of care issues go to your state government website and click on Licensing and Regulation. They will have a complete listing of citations given, the type of citation and if it's been rectified. Also, ask around. If you know someone who works in aging services, that person may tell you things "off the record" that you won't get in a formal report.

13. Once my loved one is a resident of a nursing home, what recourse do I have to express concerns about their quality of care?

First of all, follow the suggestions under the section titled "Hold People Accountable." If you can't get results on your own, you can take two routes. You can call the Ombudsman. This service is provided by your State Office on Aging. They will have a toll-free hotline number for your use. The National Long-Term Care Ombudsman Resource Center has links to all state programs (www.ltcombudsman.org). You can also call the complaint line for your State Licensing and Regulation Bureau.

14. What can we do if my parent(s)' former employer(s) is putting up barriers to claiming their pension?

This is a fast-growing problem. With mergers, acquisitions and bankruptcies, not to mention blended families and second or third marriages, deciphering a claim can become a nightmare. Many states have a Pension Rights Hotline through their Department of Aging. Usually the attorneys can't represent you in court. However, they can do research, send an initial letter of inquiry and do follow-up phone calls to help assure your rights. Many times this is effective in getting results without court proceedings. Elder Law of Michigan which operates a Pension Rights hotline reported that they had helped retirees in Kentucky, Michigan, Ohio, Pennsylvania and Tennessee recover over $3.4 million in 2008. Make sure that you trace your parent(s)' entire career path with them while their cognition is good. Otherwise you will be searching for the proverbial needle in a haystack.

15. What is Alzheimer's Disease?

"Alzheimer's disease is a brain disorder named for German physician Alois Alzheimer who first described it in 1906. Alzheimer's destroys brain cells, causing problems with memory, thinking and behavior. It is a progressive and fatal brain disease and is the most common form of dementia. Dementia is a general term for the loss of memory and other intellectual abilities. It accounts for 50-70 percent of dementia cases. (Information courtesy of Alzheimer's Association.) For information go to the www.alz.org.

16. Who are the key players in aging services and their websites?

Go to **www.youragingwelladvisor**.com and:

Administration on Aging (U.S.)   www.aoa.dhhs.gov

American Association of Homes & Services to the Aging
(AAHSA)   www.aahsa.org

Alzheimer's Association   www.info@alz.org

American Association of Retired Persons (AARP)
                                        www.aarp.org

Area Agencies on Aging   www.n4a.org

Automobile Association of America (AAA)
                                        www.aaaseniors.com

Family Caregiver Alliance   www.caregiver.org

Medicare   www.medicare.gov

National Alliance For Caregiving   www.caregiving.org

National Association of Professional Geriatric Care
Managers   www.caremanager.org

National Council on Aging   www.ncoa.org

National Family Caregivers Association
                                      www.nfcacares.org

National Guardianship Association
                                      www.guardianship.org

National Institute of Health

                                            www.nih.gov

National Long Term Care Ombudsman Center
                        www.longtermcareombudsman.org

Social Security   www.ssa.gov

Veterans Administration   www.va.gov

Wayne State Institute of Gerontology
                                      www.iog.wayne.edu

Working Caregiver Initiative   www.mywci.net

CONCLUSION

While reading this book you have learned that you are not alone. You have also learned about the types of caregivers, games people play in caregiving and strategies for success. These strategies will help you ride the waves of the Caregiver Tsunami with out falling in. I hope that you have received inspiration and assistance to help with your journey as a caregiver. I also hope that it has ignited a desire to learn more. There are many sources of information and many people available to guide you.

I'd like to leave you with one final thought: "A life cannot be measured by how many breaths you take, but rather by the moments that take your breath away."

Whatever is happening around you, remember to create those moments for yourself and your loved ones. And remember to cherish your loved ones and life. Don't let anyone or anything steal that away from you.

CPSIA information can be obtained at www.ICGtesting.com
Printed in the USA
BVOW080109111012

302665BV00001B/6/P